EASY CAMPING COCKTAILS

EASY CAMPING COCKTAILS

PRE-BATCH RECIPES
FOR TASTY, ON-THE-GO DRINKS

Tucker Ballister

ROCKRIDGE
PRESS

First Rockridge Press trade paperback edition 2022

Rockridge Press and the Rockridge Press logo are trademarks or registered trademarks of Callisto Media Inc. and/or its affiliates in the United States and other countries and may not be used without written permission.

For general information on our other products and services, please contact our Customer Care Department within the United States at (866) 744-2665, or outside the United States at (510) 253-0500.

Paperback ISBN: 978-1-68539-167-6 | eBook ISBN: 978-1-68539-593-3

Manufactured in the United States of America

Interior and Cover Designer: Lisa Forde
Art Producer: Samantha Ulban
Editor: Owen Holmes
Production Editor: Matthew Burnett
Production Manager: Jose Olivera

Photography © Thais Varela/Stocksy, p.18; StockFood / The Picture Pantry, p.36; StockFood / für ZS Verlag / Eising Studio, p.52. All Other Images Used Under License Shutterstock.

10 9 8 7 6 5 4 3 2 1 0

THIS BOOK IS DEDICATED TO ALL MY CAMPING BUDDIES.

From long-distance hikes to the shortest overnight adventures, you've proved time and again that nature's beauty is best enjoyed in the presence of great company.

_____

CONTENTS

INTRODUCTION

amping has been an essential part of my life for as long as I can remember. Some of my earliest trips were spending summers exploring the American West with my parents in our RV. Looking back, that seems like luxury compared to some of my more recent experiences. As I grew older, I took up backpacking and truck camping.

Some of my most memorable hiking trips include a full week in the Ruby Mountains of northern Nevada and a month trekking from Yosemite to Mount Whitney in California. But I've done more one- or two-day trips than I can count.

I spent most of 2021 circumnavigating the United States and living out of my Toyota Tacoma. Aside from exploring states that I had never been to, that trip afforded me the opportunity to sample local brews and seasonal fruits. It also introduced me to fellow campers who shared some of their favorite cocktail ideas with me along the way.

It made me consider how different cocktails are better for different environments. Hot toddies aren't what you're looking for in the heat and humidity of the Florida Keys, and you might not want a chilled caipirinha in your hand when huddling around a campfire on a 40°F night in the Pacific Northwest.

For me, camping has always been synonymous with kicking back and enjoying a tasty beverage. From packing whiskey in a reusable water bottle on the John Muir Trail to cooling beers in the snow on early-season backpacking trips in the Sierras, tasty camping cocktails have been essential to many of my favorite wilderness adventures.

As I've matured, the standard Rocky Mountain brews and bottom-shelf wines have lost their luster. I began to wonder: Can I enjoy more delicious and creative cocktails while I'm camping? The answer is absolutely yes.

This book began with interest in researching new cocktails for my own camping trips. It quickly grew into a comprehensive collection of classic campfire cocktails, tips to simplify on-the-go cocktail crafting efforts, and fun techniques for incorporating cocktails into camping adventures. (Responsibly. Alcohol can impair your judgment, coordination, and capacity to thermoregulate; there are some conditions in which camping and cocktails don't mix.)

I've also thrown in some ideas for scaling up cocktails if you're preparing for a large outdoor gathering. When you and your friends rent multiple neighboring campsites, for example, batching will save you from mixing drinks for the crew all night.

No good journey is without an obstacle or two. So, I had to get creative when thinking about ways to pack and prepare ingredients for specialty cocktails when refrigeration isn't an option and you don't have all the utensils you'd have in a residential kitchen.

It's a good thing that I'm not the first to consider mixing a martini or a manhattan to enjoy while sitting around the campfire. Lucky for you, we're going to enjoy our time together, learning how to spice up the drink options on your next camping trip!

CHAPTER ONE

TRAIL MIXOLOGY AND CAMPFIRE COCKTAILS

To get started, let's go over some tips that will help you camp smarter and make delicious cocktails while you're at it. From ideas for setting up an outdoor bar to the essential supplies for mixing cocktails anywhere, the tips in this chapter will help you make the recipes later in the book.

We'll go over pre-batching cocktails, talk about adapting cocktails for different types of camping, and explain the roles of things like ice and simple syrups. Bookmark this chapter, because you'll refer to it regularly as you experiment with the recipes we'll cover later.

BRINGING THE BAR OUTDOORS

Camping trips don't have to be limited to beer, wine, or whiskey stored in an insulated bottle (although that last one will always do in a pinch). But bringing the bar outdoors requires forethought.

How will you store perishable garnishes or keep ice? And what would an outdoor bar setup even look like? Do your fellow campers seriously expect you to cut limes all night?

Stepping up your camping cocktail game may require overhauling your camping equipment. Maybe you need a bigger table to set up a proper portable bar once you make camp. Or maybe you just need an upgraded beverage container for crafting larger cocktail batches in advance and adding garnishes later.

Whatever the case, you've come to the right place. We'll discuss everything you need to prepare kick-ass cocktails for car camping, RVing, and even backpacking. This book also highlights how to prep at home so there's less work to do once the fire is roaring and you're ready to kick back.

Bringing the bar outdoors isn't complicated. But operating outdoors requires proper sanitation, waste disposal, prep and cleanup, bar tool storage, and much more. Prepping exquisite camping cocktails in the wilderness presents very different challenges from what you'd find in an indoor kitchen.

Aside from sanitation, there's the all-important question of getting your ingredients to your campsite. This is going to differ depending on whether you're backpacking, car camping, or RVing, and I'll offer suggestions for each type of camping.

PRE-BATCHING COCKTAILS

Pre-batched cocktails allow you to do more of the work with the conveniences of an indoor kitchen at your disposal. Steps like mixing certain types of alcohol together can easily be done at home, even if adding certain garnishes needs to be done right before serving.

Recipes like Rum Punch (page 40) scream to be created in bulk. As long as you're able to keep the batch fresh as it travels from your house to your campsite, these recipes are designed to offer four or more servings with minimal effort once you set up camp.

Now let's talk about tips for batching your favorite cocktails.

HOW TO BATCH

Take your camping cocktails up a notch with these tips for batching.

- Multiply ingredients according to the preferred number of servings to scale up (i.e., multiply by three if your original recipe makes four servings but you need cocktails for twelve).

- Think about ingredient ratios rather than doing complex math to get exact ingredient amounts. Consider a recipe that calls for three ingredients of the following measurements: 1.5 ounces, 0.75 ounces, and 0.75 ounces. Note that comes out to a 2:1:1 ratio. When you scale up, just maintain that ratio.

- With strong ingredients, like bitters, multiply according to your desired number of servings. Then use three-fourths of that total. When batched, strong ingredients become more potent and can throw off the taste.

- Use an insulated cooler, if possible, to keep batched cocktails chilled before serving.

Ice Is Nice

Ice serves a more important role in cocktails than just cooling them down. Many cocktail recipes require ice or water to take the edge off the notes of intense ingredients, like bitters.

When you're crafting camping cocktails, you'll have to bring ice and keep it from melting. If you can't make that happen, you may need to use water as an alternative to cut cocktails and get the taste right.

There are four main types of ice used in cocktails: shaved ice, cubed ice, cracked ice, and block ice. For the purposes of camping, cubes require the least amount of work, but block ice can last longer.

If you have an ice pick and you're willing to break ice from a block as needed, this is the best option for camping cocktails. But if you want to do less work and you have a good way to keep cubed ice cold, ice cubes are an easier choice for car camping and RVing.

Of course, packing ice in a backpacking pack isn't an option if you're creating cocktails in that setting. You can, however, get creative and source snow or ice from the backcountry if it's available.

ESSENTIAL SUPPLIES

Delicious camping cocktails begin at home. This section covers the essential supplies you need for your home bar, which will help you prep ingredients, store them correctly, and mix cocktail batches that can be easily served at camp.

HOME BAR PREP ESSENTIALS

Bar spoon: For mixing cocktails and measuring a level teaspoon.

Jiggers: For measuring liquors when mixing cocktails. Two sizes work best: 1-by-2 ounces and ½-by-¾ ounce.

Mixing glass: For crafting stirred cocktails in a fancier container than the average pint glass.

Muddler: For releasing juices from fruits and herbs, such as muddling mint for a mojito.

Paring knife: For peeling, slicing, and coring fruits and vegetables, such as limes.

Peeler: For peeling fruits and herbs to make creative garnishes, such as lemon peels.

Shaker: For crafting shaken cocktails like daiquiris and sidecars. Shakers are best for cocktails containing fruit juice, dairy, or egg whites.

Strainer: For straining poured cocktails that contain only clear spirits and liqueurs.

HIT-THE-ROAD ESSENTIALS

Bar towels: For keeping your hands clean and wiping up spills.

Collapsible water storage: For transporting fresh filtered water to your campsite.

Folding table: Gives you a place to set up your bar without taking up too much space in your car.

Insulated camp mug: For serving cocktails in a safe container.

Insulated cooler: For storing perishable ingredients and keeping certain spirits cold.

Milk crate: An easy way to store and transport mixers, containers, and bar tools that don't need to be kept cold.

Tupperware set: For sealing perishable ingredients and keeping them fresh.

Simple Syrups

Simple syrup is sugar dissolved in water. It can be used in batched cocktails that are going to be stored at any temperature, and it can be added at any time.

With a shelf life of roughly a month before it gets cloudy, simple syrup is required in cocktails like mojitos, appletinis, and whiskey sours. You can buy it at most grocery or liquor stores—or you can make your own by mixing sugar and water in a saucepan, placing it over medium heat, and stirring until the sugar is dissolved. Let the syrup cool before pouring it into a glass jar, sealing the lid, and placing it in the refrigerator or on ice.

Traditionally, simple syrup is an easy 1:1 ratio of sugar to water. You can also make rich simple syrup if you need something that will last longer than a month—a 2:1 ratio of sugar to water will last for up to six months. Of course, you'll need to reduce the amount of simple syrup called for in a recipe if you're using rich simple syrup.

REFRESHER ON BAR TECHNIQUES

Even the best tools require the right skills and technique once you're actually mixing. You'll need to know the basic techniques of shaking, stirring, and straining to create the cocktails in this book correctly.

SHAKING

Shaking a cocktail serves several purposes beyond just mixing the ingredients. It also helps chill the drink, adds dilution to decrease the strength, and aerates everything to create a lighter feel. Simply:

1. Add ingredients to your shaker and fill it with ice.

2. Secure the lid.

3. Hold the shaker with one hand and the lid with the other.

4. Shake vigorously over your shoulder for a slow count of ten (or until the exterior of the shaker begins to frost).

If you don't have a shaker, you can use an insulated vacuum-sealed water bottle for the same purpose. Metal water bottles work best, but a plastic bottle will work in a pinch.

STIRRING

Cocktails are typically stirred when they only contain distilled spirits. It is also acceptable to stir cocktails when you're preparing them in the same glass they will be served in. Stirring combines the ingredients and softens the alcohol's flavor by melting the ice and slightly diluting the alcohol.

1. Chill the mixing glass or pitcher if possible. When camping, place the container in your cooler for 5 to 10 minutes before stirring. You can also

fill it with ice or cold water and stir to chill it quickly before discarding the ice or water.

2. Combine liquors and mixers and fill the container with ice to roughly two-thirds capacity.

3. Lower the bar spoon into the glass, keeping the back of the spoon against the inside of the glass, and stir around the edge of the glass to move the ice. Use mostly your fingers to stir, keeping your arm still while moving your wrist slightly.

STRAINING

Whether initially shaken or stirred, many cocktails are strained before they are served. Straining is obviously essential when you've mixed a cocktail with ice but want to serve it without ice.

Even for drinks served over ice, it is a best practice to strain out the old ice and pour the cocktail over fresh ice. This helps prevent cocktails from getting too watered down because fresh cubes last longer than those used for mixing. Straining also removes larger chunks of herbs, fruits, or spices used while shaking or stirring.

Tips for Camping with Cocktails

Preparing cocktails can be challenging at home. Doing it when you're camping on a remote mountainside will make you a legend in your friend circle. But you'll need these tips for camping with cocktails to make your backcountry bartending experience more enjoyable.

Snow better way: When you're camping in the chillier months, collecting snow in an insulated cooler is a great way to keep your cocktails cold until you're ready to serve. Even if you don't have a cooler, set anything you need to keep cold in the snow until you're mixing or serving. Clean snow can also be melted and used directly in cocktails if you're backpacking. You should just filter it first.

The river cooler: If you have a lake or riverfront campsite, place your cocktail containers or perishable ingredients in the water to keep them cool. Just make sure they are sealed in watertight containers and secured so the current doesn't take them to a lucky bystander downstream. Also, make sure the water temperature is actually cooler than the air temperature. Otherwise, this tip won't do you much good.

Stir, don't shake: This isn't saying you can't enjoy your favorite shaken cocktails while camping, but shaken cocktails generally require more cleanup. They also tend to contain more perishable ingredients with a higher likelihood of spoiling if not stored properly. If you want to play it safe, stick to stirred cocktails that contain clear liquors or spirits. Of course, these stirred cocktails can still include tasty spices that won't go bad if left unrefrigerated.

COCKTAILS FOR HOW YOU CAMP

Your camping style will determine the types of cocktails you can feasibly craft in the backcountry. Car campers, for example, can bring more supplies, and backpackers will need to get a little thriftier.

Cabin and RV campers likely have almost a full kitchen at their disposal. They will just need to pack all of the ingredients and bar tools they need to make their favorite cocktails. This book offers tips for making camping cocktails for car campers, RV and cabin campers, and backpackers.

CAR CAMPERS

Car campers love the outdoors but want to bring a little more along on their adventures than backpackers. Instead of seeking far-flung backcountry settings, car campers enjoy frontcountry camping with the ability to set up a permanent outdoor kitchen and a drink mixing station.

When planning a cocktail menu, car campers have the flexibility to bring more supplies and mix cocktails in larger batches. From mixing individual Hot Toddies (page 71) to stirring a cauldron of Spiked Hot Cocoa (page 72), car campers make it happen with ease. Plus, they don't worry about setting up and breaking down their bar daily!

WATER BOTTLE BATCHES

Premixing cocktails in water bottles lets you bring your favorite recipes on your car camping trips. Cocktails like Sangria (page 23) and Screwdriver-in-a-Bottle (page 24) go great in a thirty-two-ounce water bottle.

There are many types and sizes of water bottles out there, but insulated stainless steel bottles are best for cocktails that need to stay cold. For consistency's sake, the water bottle recipes in this book are tailored to a thirty-two-ounce bottle.

- **Bottle cork:** Save leftovers without spills.

- **Bottle/can opener:** Avoid getting too creative when opening bottles and cans.

- **Camping stove:** Great for camp cooking and essential for heating up hot camping cocktails.

- **Knife set:** Essential for cutting, coring, and paring; get a set with at least one serrated knife, a paring knife, and a chef's knife.

- **Stainless steel mugs/water bottles:** Reduce plastic waste and keep drinks insulated.

CABIN AND RV CAMPERS

Cabin and RV campers enjoy the most supplies of all campers looking to craft cocktails. Whether your cabin rental came with a fully stocked kitchen or you have your RV organized to a T, rest assured your car camping and backpacking brethren are a bit jealous of your amenities.

In this book, recipes tailored to cabin and RV campers assume access to ice, a cooler, and refrigeration. They also assume you can put more fancy touches on your cocktails than a backpacker or car camper could, such as having glassware to display your elegant preparation of the Pisco Sour (page 66).

BAR TOOLS FOR THE CABIN AND RV

- **Citrus squeezer:** Don't squeeze lemons or limes by hand when you have the drawer space in your RV or cabin for a citrus squeezer.

- **Cocktail tote:** Avoid awkwardly carrying premixed cocktails across the RV park by using a tote specifically for the occasion.

- **Glass racks:** You can bring fancier glassware in an RV, but the right rack is essential for keeping everything safe while you're driving.

BACKPACKERS

Backpackers are the minimalists of the camping world. You have to do more with less, but that doesn't mean you can't enjoy delicious cocktails in the wilderness.

Most of your cocktails will be carried in a flask or water bottle, and you'll sometimes need to rely on a water filter to get safe water for cocktails on the trail. You'll also need to use lakes, rivers, streams, and maybe even snowbanks to chill your favorite camping beverages. With a little preparation, a cocktail like the Spiked Arnold Palmer (page 38) is entirely doable for your backcountry adventures.

FLASK BATCHES

Learning how to make flask batches is essential for perfecting backpacking cocktails. For the purposes of this book, a flask is a twelve-ounce container that can serve four three-ounce servings of your desired, preferably strong, cocktail. This is different from a hip flask, which is smaller.

Most flask batches in this book can be thoroughly enjoyed at room temperature, as backpackers may not always have a way to chill their cocktails. Accordingly, many are made with aged (brown) liquor and tend to be a bit stronger than cocktails batched in water bottles or larger containers.

BAR TOOLS FOR BACKPACKERS

- **Cork multi-tool:** Gerber makes a great multi-tool for backpackers that contains a corkscrew, bottle and can openers, a foil cutter, and a pry bar.

- **Flask:** It's the lightest and most compact way to pack cocktails when you're backpacking.

- **Honey packets:** You can use these as a pick-me-up in an emergency situation or as a substitute for simple syrup in your cocktails.

- **Zip-top bags:** These are great for collecting natural ingredients, like pine needles, that can spruce up your camping cocktails.

Nature's Cocktails

One of the coolest parts about crafting cocktails in the wild is the chance to forage natural ingredients that spice things up. Including ingredients like fir or pine needles and native herbs and berries is sure to turn heads among your fellow campers.

However, I encourage everyone to forage responsibly and educate themselves on edible plants in your area. **If in doubt, leave it out.** We don't want any repeats of the infamous *Into the Wild* story.

Here are a few examples of how you might incorporate foraged ingredients into your cocktails:

▸ **Edible flowers:** Perfect for adding that final touch of garnish to your camping cocktails, whether it's adding a colorful aster to your martini or sprinkling wild bergamot over the top of your sangria.

▸ **Muddled berries:** If you're camping near an abundant batch of wild berries, responsibly collect some for use in your favorite camping cocktails, like blackberry mojitos.

▸ **Pine/fir needles:** Humans have used these in herbal teas and other beverages for thousands of years. They are loaded with vitamins and antioxidants and can even help fight off the common cold—and can be great additions to hot toddies.

ABOUT THE RECIPES

It's almost time to get crafting! To help you find the cocktails that are best for you, each recipe is labeled according to the type of camper it is intended for.

- 🚶 **Backpacker** for recipes that will primarily be batched ahead of time and stored in a flask or bottle.

- ⛺🚗 **Car Camper** for recipes that may involve a few finishing touches at the campsite but are otherwise pre-batched.

- 🏠🚐 **Cabin/RV Camper** for recipes that are campfire favorites but work best when there are more immediate resources.

Within the recipes, you'll also find tips to spice them up or make them more manageable for camping.

- **Forager tip** for suggesting a way to incorporate a new foraged element into the cocktail.

- **Mocktail tip** for opportunities to leave out the alcohol from the batched cocktail and potentially spruce up the nonalcoholic version.

- **On-the-go tip** for how best to move cocktails from your home bar to the campsite.

- **Serving tip** for variations on how to present and serve your cocktails.

Now it's time to get mixing so you can get sipping!

DEHYDRATED
BLOODY MARY,
Page 22

COCKTAIL CLASSICS

NEGRONI

TOOLS: Insulated water bottle, knife/multi-tool | **SERVES 4**

The make-ahead negroni is perfect for car camping because everything can be mixed in advance and served once you get to camp. This cocktail classic offers an enticing blend of sweetness from the vermouth and tang from the orange. It does require three different liquors, but premixing them means you only have to bring a single sealed container to store this camping cocktail.

4 ounces gin

4 ounces sweet vermouth

4 ounces Campari

1 large orange

Ice (if available)

AT HOME

Combine the gin, sweet vermouth, and Campari in an insulated water bottle. Secure the lid and shake gently. Pack in a cooler on ice. Store the orange in the cooler, too, but make sure it doesn't get squished.

AT THE CAMPSITE

To serve, fill 4 tumblers with ice (if using) or chill insulated camping mugs. Pour about 3 ounces of the prepared cocktail into each tumbler. Use a knife to create orange twists from the orange or cut the orange into wedges. Garnish each drink.

ON-THE-GO TIP: Scale this one up for large gatherings by premixing the cocktail in a large cooler and storing in several insulated growlers. Just maintain equal parts of the three liquors.

MOUNTAIN MARGARITA

TOOLS: Cocktail shaker, strainer, knife/multi-tool | **SERVES 4**

Margaritas taste just as good on a car camping trip as they do on Taco Tuesday. But embracing your time in the wilderness means getting a little creative to mix a true mountain margarita. Gatorade is great for rehydrating after a long day of exploring, and it's also a reasonable substitute for lime juice when you're mixing this delicious backcountry marg'.

Ice cubes (if available)

12 ounces tequila

8 ounces lemon-lime Gatorade

1 lime

Put ice (if using) into a cocktail shaker, then pour in the tequila and Gatorade. Shake vigorously, then strain into insulated camping mugs. Use a knife to cut the lime into wedges. Garnish each drink with a lime wedge before serving.

FORAGER TIP: If you have an edible plant expert in your company, get creative with this one and add some edible wild berries to give your margaritas a flavor that's truly unique to wherever you're camping. Start the drink by muddling the berries with a splash of water in your shaker, and then follow the recipe above.

DEHYDRATED BLOODY MARY

TOOLS: Zip-top bags, flask, water filter, camping spoon | **SERVES 6**

Let's just say that those thru-hikers you ran into last night threw down harder than you anticipated and you need something to get you going so you can still make those twenty miles you're supposed to hike. Here's your morning pick-me-up.

6 (8-ounce) packets powdered tomato paste

6 tablespoons brown sugar

2 tablespoons celery salt

2 tablespoons garlic powder

2 tablespoons black pepper

12 ounces vodka

6 packets Tabasco sauce

48 ounces water (found on trail)

1 lemon (optional)

AT HOME

Combine the tomato paste, brown sugar, celery salt, garlic salt, and black pepper in a zip-top bag and squeeze the bag to mix. Pour the vodka into a flask. Pack the Tabasco packets separately inside another zip-top bag. Carefully pack all three items in your backpack so they won't spill and/or break open. Pack a water filter.

AT THE CAMPSITE

Filter the water. Pour 2 ounces vodka into each of six camping mugs or mason jars. Divide the tomato paste mixture evenly between the mugs, then fill each three-quarters full with the filtered water. Stir with a camping spoon until the mixture dissolves. Let fellow campers add the Tabasco to taste. Taste and add more water, vodka, or Tabasco as desired. Slice the lemon and add it as a garnish (if using).

MOCKTAIL TIP: Use all water and no vodka to turn this recipe into a spicy morning pick-me-up, virgin style.

SANGRIA

TOOLS: Insulated water bottle, camping spoon | **SERVES 4**

Sweet drinks like sangria leave me feeling all sorts of sideways the next morning. But this variation on the classic recipe is perfect for relaxing after a long day of hiking without impairing your ability to do it again the next day.

1 (750ml) bottle red wine (Moscato is preferred)

4 ounces brandy (optional)

1 cup mixed fruit (frozen is easiest)

4 (0.45-ounce) packets grape drink mix powder

Ice or snow (if available)

AT HOME

Pour the wine and brandy (if using) into an insulated water bottle. Add mixed fruits and refrigerate for a minimum of four hours. Pack the bottle in a cooler on ice. Pack powdered drink packets with other dry camping goods.

AT THE CAMPSITE

Distribute the fruit mix packets to your hiking partners and have them empty the contents into their camping mugs.

Give the brandy-wine concoction a shake and fill each mug with it. Stir with a camping spoon until the fruit powder is completely dissolved. Add a handful of ice or snow (if using).

FORAGER TIP: Forage edible wild berries and add them to the water bottle as you hike to add some sweet natural flavor to your sangria.

SCREWDRIVER-IN-A-BOTTLE

TOOLS: Flask, water filter, camping spoon | **SERVES 6**

All backpackers know how hard it can be to get out of the sleeping bag in the morning. This beverage is meant to make things a little easier. Plus, it can take the edge off those throbbing knees and aching muscles until you get rolling again for another long day on the trail.

12 ounces vodka

6 packets orange powdered drink mix (such as Crystal Light or Emergen-C)

48 ounces water (found on the trail)

AT HOME

Fill a flask with vodka. Store it on the side of your pack. Pack the orange drink packets somewhere safe (such as a bear canister). Pack a water filter.

AT THE CAMPSITE

Filter the water. Pour 8 ounces of filtered water into each of six camping mugs. Pour in one orange drink packet per mug and stir with a camping spoon until it dissolves completely. Add 2 ounces of vodka. Stir gently. Sip to taste. Add more vodka or orange drink mix to achieve the desired flavor.

SERVING TIP: Crystal Light orange drink packets are a popular choice for this cocktail. To make it a little healthier, use tangerine Emergen-C packets to give your body a well-deserved vitamin C boost.

PROTEIN-PACKED WHITE RUSSIAN

TOOLS: Zip-top bags, 2 flasks, water filter, camping fork | **SERVES 6**

When you're hiking long distances, consuming enough calories to maintain muscle mass can be difficult. This White Russian, which substitutes vanilla protein powder for the cream used in the traditional recipe, helps you start your recovery at the end of a long day—deliciously.

6 tablespoons vanilla protein powder

12 ounces coffee liqueur (such as Kahlúa)

12 ounces vodka

32 ounces water (found on the trail)

AT HOME

Place the protein powder in a zip-top bag (double-bag to be safe), then pack in a safe place (such as a bear canister). Fill one flask with the coffee liqueur and another with the vodka, then secure the lids tightly. Store them safely in your pack. Pack a water filter.

AT THE CAMPSITE

Filter the water. In each of 6 camping mugs, combine 1 tablespoon of protein powder and 8 ounces of water. Stir vigorously with a camp fork to get all the lumps out (nobody likes a lumpy cocktail). Add 2 ounces of vodka and 2 ounces of coffee liqueur to each mug. Stir again and enjoy.

WHISKEY GINGER

TOOLS: Insulated water bottle, knife/multi-tool | **SERVES 4**

This is my go-to on a first date, but it's a refreshing addition to any camping trip, too. I stick to ginger ale, but some prefer to make this cocktail a bit more flavorful by using ginger beer. Either way, what we have here is a sweet whiskey-based cocktail that's easy to mix—and almost too easy to drink.

Ice (if available)

6 ounces whiskey

20 ounces ginger ale

1 lime

Fill each of four camping mugs with ice (if using). Evenly distribute the whiskey among 4 mugs and top with the ginger ale. Use a knife to cut the lime into wedges. Allow fellow campers to squeeze in juice as desired. Stir gently and enjoy.

SERVING TIP: If ice isn't accessible for this cocktail, chill the whiskey and ginger ale in your cooler or in a cold river or lake for an hour or so before serving. You can also chill your camping mug to keep your beverage cool longer.

MOJITO

TOOLS: Cocktail shaker, muddler, strainer, knife/multi-tool | **SERVES 4**

Did you know the mojito can be traced back to a sixteenth-century cocktail called El Draque? The drink was named after the English sea captain and explorer Sir Francis Drake. So, what's more appropriate when you're out exploring nature than enjoying a cool, refreshing beverage that can be linked back to one of the original explorers of the New World?

8 mint sprigs, plus 4 for garnish

2 ounces simple syrup

8 ounces white rum

3 ounces freshly squeezed lime juice

Ice cubes (if available)

Club soda

1 lime

In a cocktail shaker, combine the mint and simple syrup, then muddle them. Add the rum, lime juice, and ice (if using). Cover the shaker and shake briefly and gently. Fill each of four mugs with ice (if using). Strain the cocktail evenly into the mugs. Add the club soda to fill. Use a knife to cut the lime into wheels. Garnish each mug with a mint sprig and a lime wheel, then enjoy.

FORAGER TIP: Do a scavenger hunt around your campground to see if you can find any native mint (that you know is safe to consume) to make your regular mojito a wild foraged mint mojito.

CUBA LIBRE
TOOLS: Knife/multi-tool | **SERVES 4**

Camping is all about disconnecting from our normal routines and giving ourselves a bit of a vacation. You might think this is just a fancy name for a rum and Coke, but "a rose by any other name would [taste] as sweet." Thanks, Shakespeare. Mixing this easy cocktail once your campsite is set up will make you feel just like the name implies—*free*!

Ice (if available)

4 ounces rum

12 ounces
  Coca-Cola

1 lime

Fill each of four camping mugs with ice (if using). Add 1 ounce of rum and 3 ounces of Coke to each mug. Use a knife to cut the lime into wedges. Garnish each mug with a lime wedge. Squeeze the lime and drop it in for a little extra tang.

SERVING TIP: Pack your Cokes at the bottom of your cooler so they're nice and cold when it's time to mix this cocktail. Also, put your camping mug in your cooler for fifteen to twenty minutes before mixing to chill the mug and minimize ice consumption.

CAPE CODDER

TOOLS: Insulated water bottle, camping spoon, zip-top bag, knife/multi-tool
SERVES 6

This beverage is basically a fancy vodka-cranberry, but it's a great recipe to premix in a water bottle for backpacking trips. Great backpacking cocktails are all about simplicity, and it's hard to get any simpler than combining two ingredients. Just make sure you place that water bottle in a cool river or alpine lake for ten to fifteen minutes to chill this cocktail before enjoying.

8 ounces vodka

24 ounces cranberry juice

1 lime

Ice or snow (if available)

AT HOME

Combine the vodka and cranberry juice in an insulated water bottle. Stir to mix. Store the water bottle in the side pocket of your pack. Place the lime whole into a zip-top bag and pack it somewhere safe (such as a bear canister).

AT THE CAMPSITE

Use a knife to cut the lime into wedges. Put ice (if using) into each of six camping mugs. Pour about 5 ounces of vodka-cranberry mix into each mug. Garnish with a lime wedge, then enjoy.

ON-THE-GO TIP: When using this as a backpacking recipe, you'll want to fill your water bottle completely. Scale this recipe up to fit any insulated container by maintaining a roughly 3:1 ratio of cranberry juice to vodka.

DARK AND STORMY

TOOLS: Knife/multi-tool, camping spoon | **SERVES 4**

The name might sound brooding, but you'll be surprised by how smooth and silky this cocktail tastes. That is, if you can bring yourself to drink it once you're mesmerized by the way the setting sun brings out the golden colors in this deliciously dark drink. You can substitute ginger ale for ginger beer for this cocktail, but the rich nature of dark rum really mixes best with the stronger flavor and spicier bite of true ginger beer.

Ice (if available)

8 ounces dark rum

3 limes

20 ounces ginger beer

Put ice (if using) into each of four camping mugs. Pour 2 ounces of rum into each mug. Use a knife to halve two limes. Cut the remaining lime into wheels and set aside. Squeeze the juice of half a lime (about ½ ounce) into each mug. Add 5 ounces of ginger beer to each mug. Stir gently. Garnish each mug with a lime wheel, then enjoy.

SERVING TIP: This beverage can also be mixed without the lime juice and served with multiple lime wedges to give the drinker the ability to squeeze the lime at their discretion.

7 AND 7

TOOL: Camping spoon | **SERVES 4**

Unless you've been living on the Pacific Crest Trail your entire life, you've probably heard of this cocktail. It's one of the simplest around, but also one of the best car camping cocktails for whiskey fans. Probably the hardest thing about making this cocktail is deciding what kind of whiskey to use. It gets its name because Seagram's 7 Crown American Blended Whiskey is the traditional choice, but don't be afraid to make your own selection. Just don't sully a top-dollar scotch with lemon-lime soda!

Ice (if available)

6 ounces whiskey (such as Seagram's 7 Crown)

16 ounces lemon-lime soda (such as 7UP)

Fill each of four camping mugs with ice (if using). Pour 1½ ounces of whiskey into each mug and top with 4 ounces of soda. Stir gently and serve.

SERVING TIP: Store the whiskey and soda on ice until serving if you don't want to use ice in the drinks themselves. This allows you to enjoy a chilled cocktail while saving ice for other camping essentials.

SPICED RUM OLD-FASHIONED

TOOLS: Medium saucepan, fine-mesh sieve, lidded food container, knife/multi-tool, muddler, camping spoon | **SERVES 4**

The old-fashioned is a cocktail classic we're all familiar with; here's a spin on it. You'll learn how to make spiced simple syrup, which puts this cocktail over the top and can be used for other purposes as well. That process requires a few more kitchen appliances, which is why this cocktail is ideal for cabin or RV campers.

FOR THE SPICED SIMPLE SYRUP

1 cup sugar

1 cup water

½ teaspoon whole cloves

½ teaspoon whole black peppercorns

1 vanilla bean

1 star anise pod

1 cinnamon stick

FOR THE COCKTAIL

1 orange

6 ounces aged rum

8 dashes bitters

Ice

4 maraschino cherries (optional)

AT HOME

To make the spiced simple syrup: In a medium saucepan over medium heat, combine the sugar and water. Stir occasionally until the sugar is dissolved. Add the cloves, peppercorns, vanilla bean, star anise, and cinnamon, then reduce the heat to low. Cover and simmer for 30 minutes. Remove from the heat and strain through a fine-mesh sieve into a lidded food container. Discard the solids. Keep the simple syrup refrigerated.

AT THE CAMPSITE

To make the cocktail: Use a knife to peel four strips of peel from the orange. Put one strip into each of four camping mugs. Add 1 teaspoon of spiced simple syrup to each. Muddle thoroughly. Add 1½ ounces of rum and two dashes of bitters to each. Stir well. Add a handful of ice cubes and garnish with a maraschino cherry (if using).

ROB ROY (IN A FLASK)

TOOLS: Funnel, flask | **SERVES 4**

This camping cocktail can be completely mixed at home and then enjoyed straight from the flask while you're on the trail, so it is ideal for backpackers. You'll be able to share a taste with your fellow campers, and this one doesn't have to be served over ice to be tasty and enjoyable.

6 ounces blended scotch

3 ounces sweet vermouth

3 ounces water

6 dashes Angostura bitters

AT HOME

In a glass or camping mug, stir together the scotch, vermouth, water, and bitters. Use a small funnel to pour the cocktail into a flask, then close it. Store it safely in your pack until you get to camp.

AT THE CAMPSITE

Find a cold river or lake to safely set your flask in for 20 to 30 minutes while setting up camp. When it has chilled, pour the cocktail into camping mugs or enjoy it straight from the flask.

SERVING TIP: The longer you place your flask in cold water, the more chilled you'll be able to enjoy this cocktail. Better yet, find a snowbank if you're camping in early spring or late fall.

GINGER BEER
MOSCOW MULE,
Page 50

CHAPTER THREE

FRUITY AND SWEET COCKTAILS

SPIKED ARNOLD PALMER

TOOLS: Insulated water bottle, camping spoon | **SERVES 4**

I had a bad experience with Long Island iced teas on a high school graduation trip, so I stay away from them these days. If that's your drink of choice, I'm not one to judge, but it's not the easiest to bring into the backcountry. Enter the spiked Arnold Palmer, named after the legendary golfer, as a backpacking alternative. And if you're more of a John Daly fan, feel free to call it by that name and toast to a golfer we know enjoyed his libations!

4 packets iced tea powdered drink mix

4 packets lemonade powdered drink mix

24 ounces water

8 ounces whiskey

In an insulated water bottle, combine the iced tea mix and lemonade mix, water, and whiskey. Stir gently and secure the lid tightly. Store it safely in your pack until you get to camp, then pour into camping mugs and enjoy.

MOCKTAIL TIP: Simply leave out the whiskey to make a regular Arnold Palmer.

ON-THE-GO TIP: Scale back to a 2:1 water-to-whiskey ratio when pre-batching. Then, filter fresh water from a cool mountain stream and add about two ounces of filtered water to each mug to make this a chilled cocktail.

CHERRY VODKA PUNCH

TOOLS: Insulated water bottle, camping spoon, zip-top bag, knife/multi-tool
SERVES 4

This is a sweet and simple cocktail to prepare, but it'll pack a punch to take the edge off after your next ten-mile hike day. Of course, that'll depend on how much vodka you decide to add, but that's up to you.

4 (0.13-ounce) packets sweetened cherry drink mix powder (such as Kool-Aid)

24 ounces water

8 ounces vodka

2 lemons

Ice or snow (if available)

AT HOME

In an insulated water bottle, combine the cherry drink mix and water. Stir until the mix is dissolved completely. Add the vodka and stir again, then secure the lid tightly. Store it safely in your pack. Place the lemons whole in a zip-top bag, then pack it somewhere safe (such as a bear canister).

AT THE CAMPSITE

Using a knife, cut the lemons into quarters. Fill each of four camping mugs with about 8 ounces of the cocktail. Squeeze one-quarter of a lemon into each mug and stir. Taste and add more lemon as desired. Use any remaining lemon wedges as garnish. Add ice (if using), then serve.

RUM PUNCH

TOOLS: Insulated water bottle, water filter, camping spoon | **SERVES 5 TO 6**

This camping rum punch is about as easy and packable as it gets—the most complicated thing about it is making sure you use freshly filtered water (the colder, the better). And from there, simply combine the ingredients, stir, and enjoy!

20 ounces water, plus more found on the trail

4 packets fruit punch powdered drink mix (such as Kool-Aid)

12 ounces rum

AT HOME

In an insulated water bottle, combine the water and fruit punch drink mix. Stir until the mix is completely dissolved. Add the rum and stir again, then secure the lid tightly. Store it safely in your pack until you get to camp. Pack a water filter.

AT THE CAMPSITE

Filter some water. Pour about 2 ounces of filtered water into each of five or six camping mugs. Evenly distribute the cocktail. Stir gently and enjoy!

ON-THE-GO TIP: Scale this one up to bring as many water bottles as you need to serve your entire group. Each bottle contains roughly five to six servings. Just make sure everyone has a camping mug!

RASPBERRY LEMON DROP

TOOLS: Tall mixing glass, muddler, insulated water bottle, cocktail shaker, strainer | **SERVES 4**

The raspberry lemon drop is a great summer cocktail that you can prepare in less than five minutes. The flavor profile features the tang from the raspberry and lemon, herbal notes from the rosemary, and a bit of sweetness from the honey.

1 cup honey or brown sugar

16 ounces warm water

About 20 raspberries

8 ounces freshly squeezed lemon juice

Ice (if available)

8 ounces vodka

Rosemary or thyme sprigs (optional)

AT HOME

In a 32-ounce insulated metal water bottle, combine the honey and water, stirring until the honey is completely dissolved. Add the raspberries and muddle. Add the lemon juice, then secure the lid tightly. Shake gently to mix. Store the bottle on ice in a camping cooler.

AT THE CAMPSITE

For each cocktail, pour a quarter of the mixture into a cocktail shaker. Add 2 ounces of vodka and a handful of ice (if using). Add rosemary or thyme (if using), cap, and shake vigorously. Add two or three ice cubes to a camping mug (or chill it in the cooler for a few minutes before serving if you can't pour over ice). Strain the cocktail into the mug, then enjoy.

SPIKED STRAWBERRY-BASIL LEMONADE

TOOLS: Knife/multi-tool, cocktail shaker, muddler, strainer, 4 insulated water bottles, camping spoon | **SERVES 4**

This is one of the fruitier and more refreshing cocktails, and it's also a great candidate for a mocktail. It'll require a slightly taller camping mug than you might take backpacking, but a taller water bottle should do just fine. You'll even have the chance to add foraged strawberries if they grow in your region.

2 lemons

3 to 5 strawberry slices

5 fresh basil leaves

10 ounces lemon-lime soda (such as Sprite)

4 ounces simple syrup

8 ounces rum or vodka

Ice cubes (if available)

Use a knife to halve the lemons. Squeeze the juice from the lemons into a cocktail shaker. Add the strawberry slices and basil, then muddle. Add the lemon-lime soda, simple syrup, and ice (if using), cap, and shake vigorously 10 times. Strain the mixture into four insulated water bottles, then add 2 ounces of rum to each. Stir gently. Garnish with leftover lemon or strawberries if desired.

FORAGER TIP: If wild strawberries grow seasonally in your area, keep an eye out for them to turn this into a foraged camping cocktail.

MOCKTAIL TIP: Leave out the rum or vodka and you'll still have a super tasty and refreshing beverage.

C[LIME]B CRUSHER

TOOLS: Insulated water bottle, zip-top bag, knife/multi-tool | **SERVES 5 TO 6**

If you're a gin lover, this is the perfect cocktail to give you some old-fashioned liquid courage when you're in the backcountry. Originally developed to help mountain climbers get the confidence to send their next project, this cocktail is a refreshing and easy-to-mix option for all levels of backcountry adventures.

4 packets orange Crush Singles

24 ounces water

8 ounces gin

2 limes

Ice or snow (if available)

AT HOME

In an insulated water bottle, combine the Crush packets and water, stirring until the mix is completely dissolved. Add the gin, stir again, and secure the lid tightly. Store it safely in your pack. Place the limes whole in a zip-top bag, then pack it somewhere safe (such as a bear canister).

AT THE CAMPSITE

Using a knife, quarter the limes. Squeeze a wedge into each of five or six camping mugs. Fill the mugs with the cocktail. Use any remaining lime to swab around the rim of the mugs. Add ice (if using), then enjoy!

SNAKE IN THE GRASS

TOOLS: Insulated water bottle | **SERVES 4**

It's one of the more intriguing recipe names in this book, and it might just sneak up on you if you're not careful. That said, it's actually a super easy recipe for car camping or short backpacking trips. Go easy on the crème de menthe if you've never tried one of these cocktails before, as it can be overwhelming if you're not careful (hence, the proverbial snake!).

22 ounces lemon-lime sports drink (such as Gatorade)

8 ounces vodka

2 ounces crème de menthe

AT HOME

In an insulated water bottle, combine the sports drink, vodka, and crème de menthe, stirring until mixed thoroughly. Secure the lid tightly, then store on ice in a camping cooler.

AT THE CAMPSITE

Serve 5 to 6 ounces in each camping mug and enjoy!

FORAGER TIP: Forage for some native mint to garnish this cocktail with some native edible herbs. Just make sure you know what you're picking. If you're not 100 percent sure, you 100 percent shouldn't consume it!

MINTSUMMER NIGHT'S DREAM

TOOLS: Flask, camping spoon | **SERVES 6**

One of the best parts about this recipe is that three out of four ingredients can be wild foraged while you're hiking, which minimizes what you have to carry.

12 ounces gin

About 12 mint sprigs

3 handfuls wild berries

Water (found on the trail)

Ice or snow (if available)

AT HOME

Fill a flask with the gin, then secure the lid tightly. Store it safely in your pack until you get to camp.

AS YOU HIKE

Keep your eye out for mint (or a mint alternative) or wild berries and that you can forage.

AT THE CAMPSITE

Filter some water. Put half of a handful of wild berries and a sprig of mint into each of six camping mugs. Add a splash of filtered water. Muddle thoroughly using a camping spoon. Add 2 ounces of gin to each mug and stir gently. Serve over ice (if using), or add an extra splash of ice-cold filtered alpine stream water. Garnish with any remaining mint sprigs.

FORAGER TIP: Research the different varieties of mint and wild berries in your region to know if you can forage for those ingredients along your hike. If so, all you'll have to hike with is the gin!

RED WINE SPRITZER

TOOLS: Insulated water bottle | **SERVES 4**

This spritzer turns heavy red wine into a light, refreshing outdoor cocktail. It's super easy to mix, and you can fill a large water bottle to sip from for hours instead of returning to the bar to mix a new cocktail several times. You'll also be able to mix it in five minutes or less, so you can be ready for the next adventure when it pops up!

Ice cubes (optional)

16 ounces red wine

16 ounces club soda or lemon-lime soda

AT HOME

Fill an insulated water bottle one-quarter full with ice (if using). Add the wine, then top it off with the club soda. Secure the lid tightly, then shake gently to mix.

AT THE CAMPSITE

Serve over ice (if using) in camping mugs or sip straight from the bottle.

ON-THE-GO TIP: Don't mix this one too far in advance, or your spritzer will lose carbonation by the time you're ready to drink it.

MOCKTAIL TIP: Substitute grape juice or cranberry juice for the wine.

RIM VIEW RUM REFRESHER

TOOLS: Insulated water bottle, knife/multi-tool | **SERVES 4**

This cocktail was created with a view of Arizona's Mogollon Rim as the backdrop. It's a refreshing recipe that can be enjoyed whether you're watching the sunset over a desert landscape or the Pacific Ocean. And it includes a fruit garnish that's a bit of an outlier in the cocktail world—watermelon.

Ice cubes (if available)

12 ounces spiced rum

12 ounces melon liqueur

4 ounces freshly squeezed orange juice

4 ounces ginger ale

Watermelon (optional)

Fill an insulated water bottle halfway with ice (if using). Add the rum and melon liqueur. Top with the orange juice and ginger ale. Secure the lid tightly, then shake the bottle to mix its contents. Put a handful of ice (if using) into each mug and pour the cocktail over it. Use a knife to cut the watermelon (if using) into small wedges and garnish.

CUCUMBER LEMONADE CHILLER

TOOLS: Knife/multi-tool, cocktail shaker, muddler, strainer | **SERVES 4**

If you want to turn heads with your bartending skills on your next camping trip, look no further. This is a super crisp cocktail that your camping buddies will love, and it's got options for up to three different garnishes. You might just make a few new friends at the campground, so don't hesitate to bring extra ingredients and share!

1 cucumber

2 lemons

4 tablespoons sugar

8 mint sprigs

Ice

8 ounces water

6 ounces vodka

Lemon wedges, cucumber wedges, or mint sprigs (optional)

Using a knife, cut the cucumber into ¼-inch cubes. Juice the lemons and transfer the juice to a cocktail shaker. Add the sugar, then swirl the shaker to dissolve the sugar completely. Add the mint and cucumber and muddle.

Fill the shaker a quarter full with ice. Add the water and vodka. Cap the shaker and shake vigorously. Add ice to each of four camping mugs. Strain the cocktail into the mugs. Garnish with lemon wedges, cucumber, or mint (if using).

MOCKTAIL TIP: Just leave the vodka out of this recipe and you'll enjoy a tasty and refreshing cucumber-lemon concoction.

MINT-KISSED LEMONTINI

TOOLS: Cocktail shaker, strainer | **SERVES 4**

This camping cocktail is the perfect solution for adults and kids in your camping group. The main ingredients can be mixed into a delicious mocktail, and adults can add vodka to their mix if desired. If the kids wonder why they don't get special drinks like Mom and Dad when you're camping, this recipe gives you a safe way to give them a beverage that's out of the ordinary while still having a mix that you can use for a true cocktail!

4 tablespoons sugar

Juice of 2 lemons

16 ounces water

4 mint sprigs

6 ounces vodka

Ice cubes (if available)

In a cocktail shaker, combine the sugar and lemon juice. Swirl the shaker until the sugar dissolves completely. Add the water, mint, vodka, and a handful of ice (if using). Cap and shake vigorously. Serve neat by straining the cocktail directly into camping mugs.

SERVING TIP: Make sure the sugar is entirely dissolved in the lemon juice before adding other ingredients. A vigorous shake is essential to beat up the mint and release its aromatics.

GINGER BEER MOSCOW MULE

TOOLS: Knife/multi-tool, cocktail shaker, muddler, strainer, camping spoon
SERVES 4

Serving a Moscow mule in a copper mug is a tradition that dates back to the 1940s. Copper also has excellent insulating properties, which helps your cocktail remain chilled longer when you're camping. You may want to look into upgrading your camping mugs! The mule itself is known for its refreshing combination of lime and mint.

2 limes

Ice cubes (if available)

8 mint sprigs

8 ounces vodka

4 (12-ounce) ginger beers

Cherries or edible wild berries (optional)

Use a knife to cut the limes into wedges. Fill each of four camping mugs with ice (if using). Squeeze the juice from the lime wedges into a cocktail shaker. Add four mint sprigs and muddle. Add the vodka, cap, and shake to mix. Strain the cocktail into the camping mugs. Top with the ginger beer and stir. Garnish with the remaining mint sprigs and cherries (if using).

SERVING TIP: If you don't have a cocktail shaker, you can make this directly in your mugs using two ounces of vodka and the juice from half of a lime per mug. To muddle the mint, smack it between your (clean) hands and gently muddle in your palm using your knuckles. Smacking the mint sprig helps release the herb's aromatics before adding it to your cocktail.

HAMMOCK SNUGGLER

TOOLS: Insulated water bottle, cocktail shaker, strainer, knife/multi-tool

SERVES 4

Hammock camping is one of my favorite ways to enjoy the outdoors without worrying about setting up a tent. And if you can't find a special someone to snuggle with in your hammock, this camping cocktail serves as a great substitute. With two fruit juices and two liquors, you'll definitely want to premix this cocktail before heading out. Then just serve and sip in your hammock as the sun dips toward the horizon.

4 ounces vodka

4 ounces peach schnapps

12 ounces freshly squeezed orange juice

12 ounces cranberry juice

Ice (if available)

1 fresh peach

AT HOME

In an insulated water bottle, combine the vodka, schnapps, orange juice, and cranberry juice. Secure the lid tightly, then gently shake to mix. Store on ice in a camping cooler.

AT THE CAMPSITE

Fill a cocktail shaker halfway with ice (if using). Add a quarter of the cocktail mixture, cap, and shake vigorously. Strain the cocktail into one of four camping mugs. Repeat these steps to fill the remaining mugs. Use a knife to cut a peach into slices and garnish each mug with a slice.

ON-THE-GO TIP: Buy frozen sliced peaches to use for garnishing this cocktail instead of worrying about keeping a peach fresh and healthy. Just allow the slices to thaw a little.

PISCO SOUR, Page 66;
SIDECAR, Page 67

CHAPTER FOUR

SOUR AND TART COCKTAILS

GOLD RUSH

TOOLS: Small saucepan, cocktail shaker, strainer, knife/multi-tool
SERVES 4

For whiskey lovers, the gold rush is a camping spin on a classic whiskey sour. It's an excellent cocktail for cabin campers or RVers who have a few more amenities at their disposal. The recipe substitutes honey syrup for simple syrup, which adds more nuance and richness.

FOR THE HONEY SYRUP

½ cup honey

½ cup water

FOR THE COCKTAIL

8 ounces bourbon

4 ounces freshly squeezed lemon juice

Ice cubes

1 lemon

AT HOME

To make the honey syrup: In a small saucepan over medium heat, combine the honey and water. Cook, stirring, for 1 to 2 minutes, until the honey is fully dissolved, then immediately remove it from the heat. Don't allow the solution to simmer. Cool to room temperature before using and store in a sealed container in the refrigerator for up to 1 month. Store on ice in a camping cooler.

AT THE CAMPSITE

To make the cocktail: In a cocktail shaker, combine the bourbon, lemon juice, and 3 ounces honey syrup. Fill the shaker halfway with ice, cap, and shake vigorously. Add ice to each of four camping mugs. Strain the cocktail into the mugs. Use a knife to cut the lemon into wedges, then garnish each mug with a wedge.

RED GRAPEFRUIT FIZZ

TOOLS: Insulated water bottle, zip-top bag, cocktail shaker, knife/multi-tool
SERVES 4

This sour cocktail is a delight for citrus lovers, as it includes not only grapefruit but also orange and lime. It has plenty of tartness, but the cranberry and club soda take the edge off to create a mild and refreshing afternoon beverage. If you do a little prep work at home, mixing this cocktail at your campsite is a breeze.

4 Ruby Red grapefruit

4 oranges

4 limes

8 ounces cranberry juice

8 ounces vodka or gin

Ice (if available)

8 ounces club soda

AT HOME

Juice the grapefruit, oranges, and half of the limes into an insulated water bottle. Add the cranberry juice and vodka. Seal the lid tightly and shake gently to mix. Store on ice, along with club soda, in a camping cooler. Place the remaining two limes in a zip-top bag and store.

AT THE CAMPSITE

Fill a cocktail shaker with ice (if using). Add the cocktail, cap, and shake vigorously. Fill each of four camping mugs with ice. Strain the cocktail into mugs, then top with the club soda. Use a knife to cut the remaining limes into wedges. Garnish each mug with a wedge, then serve.

SOUR SHANDY

TOOLS: Insulated water bottle, knife/multi-tool, lidded food container
SERVES 6

It doesn't get much easier than mixing your favorite sour beer with a shot of your preferred clear spirit and a little fruit juice. Sour beers on the lighter end of the spectrum are better for a refreshing beer shandy.

6 ounces clear spirit of choice

6 ounces freshly squeezed fruit juice (lemon, lime, or grapefruit)

1 orange

6 (12-ounce) light sour beers of choice

Ice

AT HOME

In an insulated water bottle, combine the spirit and fruit juice, then secure the lid tightly. Use the knife to slice the orange, and store it in a lidded food container. Store the bottle, container, and beer in a camping cooler on ice.

AT THE CAMPSITE

Pour 2 ounces of the cocktail into each of six camping mugs. Top with a sour beer poured gently at a 45-degree angle to minimize the head. Garnish with an orange slice and enjoy.

ON-THE-GO TIP: Avoid the use of camping mugs altogether by cracking open your beer, taking a few sips, adding your mixer directly to the can or bottle, and giving it a gentle swirl. It might not be fancy, but it'll get the job done!

GREYHOUND

TOOLS: Insulated water bottle, lidded food container, knife/multi-tool, camping spoon | **SERVES 4**

The greyhound can be mixed about as quickly as its namesake can get on a scent and be off. Perfect for a warm summer day, this cocktail is a great substitute for a mimosa and much lighter than a Bloody Mary if you're getting your drinking day started before noon!

4 Ruby Red grapefruit

8 ounces vodka or gin

Ice (if available)

2 limes

AT HOME

Squeeze the juice from the grapefruit into an insulated water bottle. Add the vodka. Secure the lid tightly, then shake to mix. Store on ice in a camping cooler. Pack the limes whole in a lidded food container in the cooler.

AT THE CAMPSITE

Use a knife to cut the limes into wheels. Fill each of four camping mugs with ice (if using). Pour the cocktail over the ice and stir gently. Garnish with a lime wheel and enjoy.

ON-THE-GO TIP: As an alternative to juicing fresh grapefruit, simply buy grapefruit juice, but look for a brand with as little added sugar as possible. Use twenty-four ounces of grapefruit juice to maintain a 3:1 mixer-to-alcohol ratio.

THE FRENCH TART

TOOLS: Small saucepan, fine-mesh strainer, lidded food container, insulated water bottle, cocktail shaker, strainer | **SERVES 4**

This light, tart cocktail offers a unique blend of rosemary, grapefruit, and gin. But it also includes a less widely used elderflower liqueur that gives it a taste you'll seldom find elsewhere.

FOR THE ROSEMARY SIMPLE SYRUP

1 cup water

1 cup sugar

4 to 6 rosemary sprigs

FOR THE COCKTAIL

6 ounces freshly squeezed grapefruit juice (about 1 grapefruit)

1 ounce freshly squeezed lemon juice (about 1 lemon)

4 ounces elderflower liqueur (such as St-Germain)

8 ounces gin

8 dashes sage bitters, plus more as needed

Ice

AT HOME

To make the rosemary simple syrup: In a small saucepan over high heat, bring the water to a boil. Add the sugar, stirring until dissolved. Add the rosemary and let boil for 1 minute. Remove from the heat and let steep for 30 to 60 minutes. Pour the syrup through a fine-mesh strainer into a lidded food container.

To make the cocktail: In an insulated water bottle, combine the grapefruit juice, lemon juice, elderflower liqueur, gin, 2 ounces of rosemary simple syrup, and the bitters. Secure the lid and shake gently to mix. Store in a camping cooler on ice.

AT THE CAMPSITE

Fill a cocktail shaker with ice. Add the cocktail, cover, and shake to chill. Taste and add more bitters as desired. Strain into camping mugs and enjoy.

GIN SOUR

TOOLS: Cocktail shaker, strainer | **SERVES 4**

This cocktail is a twist on the familiar whiskey sour. It's like a Tom Collins—minus the soda—which means the quality of the gin you choose does matter. Go for a middle-to-top-shelf brand for this cocktail, like Tanqueray No. Ten.

8 ounces gin

4 ounces freshly squeezed lemon juice

2 teaspoons superfine sugar

Ice (if available)

Orange slices or maraschino cherries (optional)

In a cocktail shaker, combine the gin, lemon juice, and sugar. Add a handful of ice (if using). Cover and shake until chilled. Strain into each of four camping mugs. Garnish each mug with an orange slice (if using) and enjoy.

ON-THE-GO TIP: If you're short on ice that's safe to use for this cocktail, just make sure you keep all the ingredients, plus your camping mugs, chilled in your cooler until you're ready to mix and serve.

APPLE SWEET TART

TOOLS: Cocktail shaker, strainer, knife/multi-tool | **SERVES 4**

This cocktail will take you back to your middle school sweet-and-tart candy days. This blend of vodka and sour apple schnapps is ideally presented in a martini glass, but because we're talking about camping cocktails, an insulated camping mug will do just fine.

2 lemons

6 ounces of vodka

6 ounces of sour apple schnapps

3 ounces simple syrup

Ice (if available)

1 green apple

Chill four camping mugs in a camping cooler. Squeeze the juice of the lemons into a cocktail shaker. Add the vodka, schnapps, and simple syrup. Add ice (if using), cover, and shake vigorously to chill and combine. Strain the cocktail into the chilled camping mugs. Use a knife to slice the apple. Garnish each mug with a slice and enjoy.

SERVING TIP: If you're running out of ice on your camping trip, add two ounces of cold water to your shaker before covering and shaking.

KILLER TROPICAL CHAI

TOOLS: Knife/multi-tool, kitchen scale, medium bowl, strainer, lidded food container, zester, small saucepan, camping spoon, squirt bottle, insulated water bottle | **SERVES 4**

This chai-infused cocktail is a blend of tropical flavors and the tart notes that you often crave after a long day outdoors. It's more labor intensive than other camping cocktails, but a lot of the preparation can be done in your home kitchen.

FOR THE CHAI-INFUSED WHISKEY

1 chai tea bag

1 (750ml) bottle whiskey

FOR THE PINEAPPLE SYRUP

1 small pineapple

Sugar, as needed

FOR THE LEMON SIMPLE SYRUP

4 lemons

Sugar, as needed

FOR THE COCKTAIL

20 drops cardamom bitters

8 dashes pineapple serrano bitters
 (if unavailable, Angostura bitters)

20 ounces mandarin mixer

Ice (if available)

Dried orange or pineapple (optional)

Cinnamon stick (optional)

Star anise pod (optional)

AT HOME

To make the chai-infused whiskey: Dip the tea bag in hot water, then place it in the bottle of whiskey. Steep for 10 to 15 minutes, then remove and discard the tea bag. Let the infused whiskey rest for 10 to 14 days for the flavor to deepen into the spirit.

To make the pineapple syrup: Use a knife to peel a pineapple and cube it. Weigh the pineapple cubes. Weigh out an equal amount of sugar and put both the pineapple and sugar in a medium bowl. Cover the bowl and allow it to sit on the counter for 6 to 12 hours, or until syrup fills the bottom of the bowl. Strain the syrup into a lidded food container and store in the refrigerator.

To make the lemon simple syrup: Use a zester to zest one lemon, then set aside. Squeeze the juice from all four lemons into a small saucepan (you should have about ½ cup). Add an equal amount of sugar, then place over medium heat. Cook, stirring and maintaining a low simmer (reducing the heat as necessary) until the sugar is dissolved. Reduce the heat to low, add the lemon zest, stir, and allow it to sit for 5 minutes. Remove from heat and steep for 45 minutes. Strain the simple syrup into a reusable squirt bottle, then store in the refrigerator. Discard the solids.

To prep the cocktail: In an insulated water bottle, combine 6 ounces of infused whiskey, 2 ounces of pineapple syrup, 1 ounce of lemon syrup, the cardamom and pineapple bitters, and mandarin mixer. Secure the lid, then shake gently to mix. Store on ice in a camping cooler.

AT THE CAMPSITE

Fill four camping mugs halfway with ice (if using). Shake the water bottle to mix the contents. Pour the cocktail over the ice and stir gently. Garnish with a dried orange, cinnamon stick, or star anise (if using).

GINGER CLEMENTINE OLD-FASHIONED

TOOLS: Knife/multi-tool, cocktail shaker, muddler, camping spoon, strainer
SERVES 4

This is a tart twist on the old-fashioned that isn't too tough for car campers to pull off. It features fresh ginger and a peeled clementine to provide notes of citrus. Boozy cherries are a fun addition for garnish, and I'm sure you'll find yourself eating one or two on their own!

4 clementines, peeled and sliced

Knob fresh ginger

4 boozy maraschino cherries (such as Luxardo), plus more for garnish

8 dashes bitters of choice

8 ounces rye whiskey

Ice (if available)

Use a knife to peel the clementines and ginger. Slice the clementines. Cut eight thin slices of ginger. In a cocktail shaker, combine the clementines, ginger, cherries, and bitters. Muddle thoroughly. Add the whiskey and ice (if using). Stir to chill and combine all ingredients. Fill each of four camping mugs with ice (if using). Strain the cocktail into the mugs. Garnish each with a cherry.

THE BLIZZARD (CRANBERRY BOURBON)

TOOLS: Insulated water bottle, cocktail shaker, strainer | **SERVES 5 TO 6**

This bourbon-centric cocktail is ideal for winter camping, and it's best enjoyed around a roaring campfire. A nice mix of bourbon, cranberry juice, and freshly squeezed lemon juice give it plenty of tartness, but the dash of simple syrup helps smooth things out. Look for unsweetened or diet cranberry juice to get the tartness right in this cocktail.

13.5 ounces bourbon

9 ounces unsweetened cranberry juice

6 ounces simple syrup

3 ounces freshly squeezed lemon juice

Ice (if available)

Lemon slices and cranberries (optional)

AT HOME

In an insulated water bottle, combine the bourbon, cranberry juice, simple syrup, and lemon juice. Secure the lid tightly, then shake gently to mix. Store on ice in a camping cooler.

AT THE CAMPSITE

Fill a cocktail shaker halfway with ice (if using), then add the cocktail. Cap and shake vigorously. Add ice to five or six camping mugs. Strain the cocktail into the mugs. Garnish with lemon slices and cranberries (if using) and enjoy.

PISCO SOUR

TOOLS: Cocktail shaker, strainer | **SERVES 4**

You get the balance of sour from the lime, a hint of sweetness from the simple syrup, the complexity of the bitters, and a unique frothy texture from the addition of the egg white. Yes, this may be a little unexpected for most campers, but it's totally within the realm of possibility for cabin campers or RVers. You can even use your bitters to create a unique design in the foam before serving.

8 ounces pisco

4 ounces freshly squeezed lime juice

2 ounces simple syrup

4 large egg whites

Ice

Bitters of choice

In a cocktail shaker, combine the pisco, lime juice, simple syrup, and egg whites. Cover and shake for 15 seconds. Add ice to the shaker, cover, and shake for another 30 seconds. Strain the cocktail into camping mugs. Foam will collect at the top as you pour. Add three dashes of bitters to the foam in each mug, then serve.

SERVING TIP: The initial shake without ice is essential for this cocktail, as it allows foam from the egg to form before it can be diluted. The second shake (with ice) chills your drink and strengthens the foam so you'll be able to draw your own bitters designs on that frothy top layer once you pour it.

SIDECAR

TOOLS: Insulated water bottle, knife/multi-tool, small bowl, cocktail shaker, strainer | **SERVES 8**

This classic cocktail traces its origins back to World War I. Apparently, the U.S. army captain who invented the cocktail was known for riding around in a motorcycle side-car (maybe so he didn't have to drive after enjoying his signature creation).

16 ounces cognac (VS or VSOP, whichever you prefer)

8 ounces Cointreau

8 ounces freshly squeezed lemon juice

Ice

1 lemon

Sugar, to coat rim (optional)

8 dashes bitters (optional)

AT HOME

In an insulated water bottle, combine the cognac, Cointreau, and lemon juice. Secure the lid tightly, then shake gently to mix. Store on ice in a camping cooler.

AT THE CAMPSITE

Use a knife to cut the lemon into wedges. Run a wedge around the rims of eight camping mugs (or glasses). Pour sugar (if using) into a small bowl and dip the mugs into the sugar to coat the rims. Put a handful of ice into a cocktail shaker. Add the cocktail, cover, and shake vigorously. Strain the cocktail into the mugs, add a dash of bitters to each (if using), garnish with the lemon wedges, and serve.

SPIKED
HOT COCOA,
Page 72

HOT AND FROZEN COCKTAILS

WHISKEY CIDER

TOOLS: Flask, water filter, camping stove and pot, camping spoon
SERVES 5 TO 6

For a backpacking cocktail, it doesn't get much simpler than adding whiskey to hot apple cider. The bourbon will work its magic on your aches and pains after a long day of hiking. As long as you have space in your pack for a flask and a few cider packets, this is an easy one to bring on short or long backpacking adventures.

12 ounces bourbon

6 packets spiced apple cider powdered drink mix

48 ounces water (found on the trail)

Cinnamon sticks (optional)

AT HOME

Fill a flask with bourbon and store it safely in your pack. Pack the apple cider packets and store them somewhere safe (such as a bear canister). Pack a water filter.

AT THE CAMPSITE

Filter the water. In a pot over a camping stove, bring the water to a boil. Add the apple cider packets and stir until completely dissolved. Let the cider cool for 1 to 2 minutes, then pour it into five or six camping mugs. Top each with 2 ounces of bourbon. Stir with a cinnamon stick (if using) or camping spoon. Leave the cinnamon stick in for a little spice before enjoying.

HOT TODDY

TOOLS: Camping stove and pot, knife/multi-tool, camping spoon
SERVES 4

A hot toddy is a great cocktail for everything from après-ski hangouts to helping you get over a slight cold. It's also super easy to make on car camping trips as long as you have a camping stove, propane, and a pot big enough to mix all the ingredients.

2 lemon-ginger tea bags

16 to 20 ounces water

1 lemon

10 ounces whiskey

2 packets spiced apple cider powdered drink mix (optional)

4 cinnamon sticks (optional)

3 ounces honey (optional)

Place the tea bags and water in a camping pot and bring to a boil on a camping stove. Remove the pot from the heat when it reaches a boil. Use a knife to cut the lemon into four wedges, then squeeze the juice from the wedges into the pot. Add the rind from one lemon wedge. Add the whiskey and the apple cider drink mix, cinnamon stick, and/or honey (if using). Stir occasionally for several minutes as you allow the mixture to cool. Pour into camping mugs when you're ready to serve.

SERVING TIP: If you bring maple syrup for morning pancakes on your camping trip, substitute it for the honey to create an even richer and sweeter hot toddy.

SPIKED HOT COCOA

TOOLS: Camping stove and pot | **SERVES 4**

Hot chocolate is a campfire classic, but experienced campers can get sick of a cocoa packet dissolved in water after the first dozen times. So, this cocktail gives you a way to spice up your hot cocoa offering on your next car camping trip. By adding a little tequila (though it really is dealer's choice on the liquor you add), stirring with a cinnamon stick, and garnishing with a dash of cayenne pepper, you'll add a fresh kick to a camping classic.

32 ounces water

4 packets hot chocolate powdered drink mix

4 cinnamon sticks

8 ounces tequila

4 marshmallows (optional)

4 pinches ground cayenne pepper

In a camping pot on a camping stove, bring the water to a boil. Remove the pot from the heat and add the hot chocolate mix. Stir with the cinnamon sticks until the hot chocolate powder is completely dissolved. Add the tequila and stir again. Pour into four camping mugs and add one marshmallow to each (if using), letting them melt on top for a float. Garnish each mug with a pinch of cayenne pepper and a cinnamon stick, then enjoy.

MOCKTAIL TIP: There's nothing wrong with leaving out the tequila to enjoy a mocktail that's a little fancier than just dissolving a hot cocoa packet in hot water.

IRISH INSTA-COFFEE

TOOLS: Flask, water filter, camping stove and pot, camping spoon
SERVES 6

On those days when you don't have to cover a lot of mileage, enjoy a slow morning and take the edge off with a morning cocktail like this one. If you already have your camping stove set up to make morning oatmeal, just boil a second batch of water to make this camping cocktail.

12 ounces of your preferred Irish whiskey

6 packets instant coffee of choice

48 ounces water (found on the trail)

AT HOME

Place the whiskey in a flask and store it safely in your pack. Pack the instant coffee somewhere safe (such as a bear canister). Pack a water filter.

AT THE CAMPSITE

Filter the water. In a camping pot on a camping stove, bring the water to a boil. Mix in the instant coffee and remove the pot from the heat. Stir thoroughly to dissolve the coffee and let sit for 1 to 2 minutes to cool. Pour the coffee into six camping mugs and top each with 2 ounces of whiskey. Stir gently to mix.

MOUNTAIN BUZZ

TOOLS: 2 flasks, water filter, camping stove and pot, camping spoon
SERVES 8 TO 12

This hot cocktail is ideally enjoyed around an evening campfire, but it'll also give you a kick of caffeine and liquor to get your day started on your next backpacking trip. It can be made over a simple backpacking stove, and you'll just need to pack in the liquors in flasks. Plus, you get to choose your favorite flavor of instant coffee.

12 ounces coffee liqueur (such as Kahlúa)

12 ounces spiced rum

6 packets instant coffee of choice

Marshmallows (optional)

48 ounces water (found on the trail)

AT HOME

Fill one flask with the coffee liqueur and the other with the rum. Store them safely in your pack. Pack the instant coffee and marshmallows (if using) somewhere safe (such as a bear canister). Pack a water filter.

AT THE CAMPSITE

Filter the water. In a camping pot on a camping stove, bring the water to a boil. Remove the pot from the heat and add the instant coffee. Stir thoroughly and allow it to cool for 2 to 3 minutes. Pour the coffee into 8 to 12 camping mugs and top them off with equal parts coffee liqueur and rum. Add the marshmallows (if using) and enjoy.

SERVING TIP: Roast the marshmallows and pop one or two right into your cocktail to give it a true camping touch.

FROZEN COCONUT MOJITO

TOOLS: Blender, knife/multi-tool | **SERVES 4**

The perfect balance between a minty mojito and a tropical piña colada, this frozen coconut mojito is an absolutely refreshing cocktail for scorching summer camping trips. The mint accompanies the coconut, rum, and lime juice exceptionally well.

64 ounces ice

8 ounces coconut rum

8 ounces cream of coconut

4 limes

16 fresh mint leaves

Place the ice in a blender. Add the rum, then add the cream of coconut. Use a knife to halve the limes, then squeeze in the juice (about 4 ounces). Add 12 mint leaves. Cap the blender and blend until the mixture is completely smooth. Pour into four camping mugs and garnish with the remaining mint leaves.

MOCKTAIL TIP: Substitute coconut water for the coconut rum to turn this into an equally refreshing, but alcohol-free, mocktail.

WINE SLUSHY

TOOLS: Ice cube trays, blender, insulated water bottle | **SERVES 4**

Although making your own slushy from wine requires more advance preparation than some other camping cocktails, it's the perfect way to turn your favorite red wine into a refreshing summer cocktail. Plus, when summer turns up the heat, this cocktail will be less dehydrating than drinking straight wine.

1 (750ml) bottle red wine of choice

AT HOME
The night before you leave on your trip, pour the wine into ice cube trays and freeze it for a minimum of 4 hours. When the cubes are solid, take them out of the trays and drop them into a blender. Pulse and blend until the cubes are crushed and the mixture is slushy. Pour the drink into an insulated water bottle and refrigerate. Store on ice in your camping cooler until you get to your campsite.

AT THE CAMPSITE
Take the bottle out of the cooler 15 to 30 minutes before you want to serve (depending on the outside temperature). Then, pour into camping mugs and enjoy.

FROZEN MUDSLIDE

TOOLS: Blender | **SERVES 4**

A frozen mudslide is a delicious cocktail and a filling camping dessert in one package. The ingredients require a refrigerator, and you'll need electricity to run your blender, but cabin campers and RVers can definitely impress their guests with this cocktail. The dairy can be replaced with coconut ice cream or dairy-free vanilla yogurt.

32 ice cubes

8 to 12 scoops vanilla ice cream

4 ounces vodka

4 ounces Irish cream (such as Baileys)

4 ounces coffee liqueur (such as Kahlúa)

4 ounces chocolate syrup

Whipped cream (optional)

Chocolate sprinkles (optional)

In a blender, combine the ice cubes, ice cream, vodka, Irish cream, coffee liqueur, and chocolate syrup. Cap the blender and blend until smooth. Pour the cocktail into four camping mugs and freeze them for 5 to 10 minutes to thicken. Top with whipped cream and/or chocolate sprinkles (if using) and enjoy.

SERVING TIP: Experiment with this mudslide recipe by changing up the type of ice cream you use in the initial step. Vanilla is always a safe bet, but don't be afraid to try other flavors.

FROSÉ

TOOLS: Microwave-safe glass jar, mason jar, camping spoon, fine-mesh sieve, 1-gallon zip-top bag, large dish, blender, insulated water bottle

SERVES 4

This recipe takes the simplicity of the wine slushy and fancies it up. It still requires planning, but it's a great alternative if you don't like sweet cocktails, such as daiquiris or margaritas. Plus, you can do the prep work the night before and enjoy a refreshing cocktail the next day.

FOR THE STRAWBERRY SIMPLE SYRUP

½ cup water

½ cup sugar

1 cup chopped strawberries

FOR THE COCKTAIL

1 (750ml) bottle rosé wine (the darker, the better)

½ cup vodka

AT HOME

To make the strawberry simple syrup: In a microwave-safe glass jar, combine the water and sugar, then microwave for 1 to 2 minutes, or until boiling. Stir the mixture until the sugar dissolves. Add the strawberries and refrigerate overnight. In the morning, strain the mixture through a fine-mesh sieve into a mason jar, then secure the lid. Discard the solids and keep the syrup refrigerated.

To make the cocktail: Pour the wine into a 1-gallon zip-top bag and set it in a large dish or food container. Freeze overnight. In the morning, transfer the frozen wine to a blender. Add the vodka and 4 tablespoons of strawberry simple syrup. Blend until smooth. Taste and add more simple syrup as desired. Pour the cocktail into an insulated water bottle and store on ice in a cooler until you reach your campsite.

AT THE CAMPSITE

Pour the cocktail into four camping mugs or enjoy it straight from the bottle!

FORAGER TIP: If you're camping during the right season, forage for local strawberries as a garnish.

ON THE GO TIP: Once mixed, pour the cocktail into a soft plastic water bottle and place it back in the freezer. As long as the bottle can expand slightly without cracking, this will keep your frosé ice cold when you need to travel farther to reach your campsite.

THE DIRTY BANANA

TOOL: Blender | **SERVES 4**

The name might not sound all that appealing, but you'll be pleasantly surprised by this frozen final creation. The final product is basically a delicious banana split in a glass with a kick of alcohol. Although the recipe calls for vodka, you can easily use rum instead if that's your preference.

8 ounces crushed ice

6 ounces vodka

4 ounces coffee liqueur (such as Kahlúa)

4 frozen ripe bananas

4 ounces heavy cream

4 ounces cream of coconut

Chocolate syrup (optional)

Maraschino cherries (optional)

In a blender, combine the ice, vodka, coffee liqueur, bananas, cream, and cream of coconut. Cap the blender and blend until smooth. Squeeze chocolate syrup (if using) around the inside of four camping mugs. Pour the cocktail into the mugs. Top with maraschino cherries (if using) and drink umbrellas (also optional).

MEASUREMENT CONVERSIONS

VOLUME EQUIVALENTS (DRY)

US STANDARD	METRIC (approximate)
⅛ teaspoon	0.5 mL
¼ teaspoon	1 mL
½ teaspoon	2 mL
¾ teaspoon	4 mL
1 teaspoon	5 mL
1 tablespoon	15 mL
¼ cup	59 mL
⅓ cup	79 mL
½ cup	118 mL
⅔ cup	156 mL
¾ cup	177 mL
1 cup	235 mL
2 cups or 1 pint	475 mL
3 cups	700 mL
4 cups or 1 quart	1 L
½ gallon	2 L
1 gallon	4 L

VOLUME EQUIVALENTS (LIQUID)

US STANDARD	US STANDARD (ounces)	METRIC (approximate)
2 tablespoons	1 fl. oz.	30 mL
¼ cup	2 fl. oz.	60 mL
½ cup	4 fl. oz.	120 mL
1 cup	8 fl. oz.	240 mL
1½ cups	12 fl. oz.	355 mL
2 cups or 1 pint	16 fl. oz.	475 mL
4 cups or 1 quart	32 fl. oz.	1 L
1 gallon	128 fl. oz.	4 L

RESOURCES

***Backpacker Radio* podcast:** A great resource for folks interested in long-distance hiking and backpacking. Includes gear recommendations and fun stories from the trail.

***The Backpack Guide* blog:** A useful website with gear reviews, hiking tips, and trail recommendations. Find it at thebackpackguide.com.

***Camping World* blog:** Includes articles on everything from the basics of RVing to comprehensive gear guides to deep dives on America's national parks and how to plan trips to them. Find it at blog.campingworld.com.

***The Campout Cookbook*:** A great resource to spice up camping meals and give you something delicious to pair with your favorite cocktails from this book.

***Deep Survival*:** One of my all-time favorite books about wilderness survival and the psychology of who survives, and why, in search-and-rescue situations.

***The Dirtbag Diaries* podcast:** An awesome listen to learn about new places to camp, how to plan trips, and sometimes, how to avoid doing all the wrong things when recreating outdoors.

Edible Wild Plants: A North American Field Guide to Over 200 Natural Foods: An excellent resource if you're interested in learning more about what you can forage to add to your camping cocktails.

Into Thin Air: An iconic book about disaster and survival on Mount Everest. Maybe not the place you'd be mixing a complex camping cocktail, but an inspiring and harrowing tale nonetheless.

Leave No Trace: A website that helps you study up on the seven principles of outdoor ethics to minimize your impact on future camping trips and make sure we take care of our favorite wilderness areas for generations to come. Find it at lnt.org.

The Wayward Home: An excellent online resource for all things related to van life, RV living, truck camping, and much more. Find it at thewayward-home.com.

INDEX

D

ACKNOWLEDGMENTS

I'd like to thank my parents and brother for creating the support system that has allowed me to push my limits and explore new places. Knowing I have a stable home to return to if needed has driven me to take chances I otherwise wouldn't have. Consequently, those chances have led to many memorable experiences I'll never forget. I'd also like to thank my family members around the country for welcoming me on my five-month spirit quest around the United States in 2021. Without knowing I had safe places to stay within a few days' drive, I would've given up several times over. Finally, I'd like to thank my friends. I'm incredibly blessed to have you in my life. From giving me the motivation to get outside to listening and talking through life's big questions over a tasty beverage, you've always had my back and it means the world to me!

ABOUT THE AUTHOR

Tucker Ballister is a full-time writer for *Camping World* and his blog, *The Backpack Guide*. He grew up hiking, kayaking, and swimming in alpine lakes in the Sierra Nevada north of Lake Tahoe. His favorite trips include truck camping throughout the United States, backpacking the John Muir Trail, and traversing the Ruby Mountains in Northern Nevada. Wherever his adventures lead, he loves kicking back and enjoying a refreshing beverage at the end of a long day. He thinks those beverages are a little more satisfying when you earn them, though!

CPSIA information can be obtained
at www.ICGtesting.com
Printed in the USA
JSHW011737250722
28423JS00001B/4

9 781685 391676